Musings Of A Midwestern Millenial

Struggles from a Working Class American Woman

Shelby Eschker

Dedication

To Working Class Women-

You are inspirational.

Preface

Somewhere along the path of progress, we severed our connection with the planet, ourselves and our community. Watching the citizens of the United States of America, particularly those in the working class, increasingly struggle to provide ends meet has stirred a deep demand for justice. Citizens rights, particularly those of women and minority groups, are consistently threatened. Our planet is drained time and time again, not for the benefit of the masses but for the profit of a few. This collection hopes to convey some of the emotions of the American plight.

Acknowledgements

I want to acknowledge my parents, my son and my friends for always pushing me outside of my comfort zone, and for always believing I'll succeed.

Thank you to the working class. Your strength, resolve and perseverance are inspirational.

Thank you for the fierce, determined and resourceful women who fought (and continue to fight) for my rights.

Thank you to indigenous people, whose stewardship of this land is unparalleled.

Thank you to Mother Earth, who does not received the recognition nor respect she deserves.

1. Beyond the Ocean Gate

A billionaire will
send submarines in the sea
of working class tears.

2. The Ant Hill Metropolis

I often wonder what it'd be like,
To live as a bug, with freedom of flight?
Adventurous and curious, to fly carefree
To buzz about flowers consumed with glee.
Taking in views from the heavenly skies
Enjoying sweet treats as hunger arises.

But is it safe, is the area clear?
Freedom comes with the fear that danger is near
Will the bug swatter rage down from a towering hand,
Sending me hurling into the land?

Or perhaps the sweet treat, a delight to my taste
Is filled with poison that will cause me to waste
Until all that remains is a shell with no soul
The destruction of venom taking its toll.

I guess it's not different, human or bug
Whether a middle class worker or a garden slug.
Mortality strikes and logic conquered by fear
The blanket of comfort withered and sheer
I can cease to wonder what it'd be like,
The bugs and the humans share the same plight.

3. Corporate Antichrist

Two hundred million health insurance claims
Are denied every day. Cancer patients are
Drained of every dollar they have,
Sacrificing every ounce of material possession
Just at a hope of living another day;
One more laugh with friends,
One more "I love you"
One more favorite breakfast at a local diner
One more episode of that show they can't stop watching
Meanwhile, CEO's worry about which second vacation
home to buy,
What market to monopolize and steal
What personal staff they can add to their collection,
Which yacht they prefer to spread toxins into the seas
All with the blood money they gain by sacrificing the
souls of the helpless.

4. Inner Conflict

Maybe I should lose weight?
Everyone is doing that diet.
Do you think this shirt makes me look fat?
I just want to be accepted.
All I see is criticism of women
I don't want to end up like them, do I?
Stamped with their own scarlet letter.
Ferocious and free
Actually, nevermind
Keep the diets, the fads, the pills
Everyone deserves love no matter the size.

5. Purple People

The Red against the Blue
Bitter and estranged foes
Both believe themselves to be true
Each side the cause of the others woes.

But the purple people know
The war is not amongst ourselves
Those from the upper stir down below
Pulling dissonance off the shelves

This recipe for dissension
Which enrages and confounds
Sowing internal tension
Predators lurk in the background

The purple people understand
There is no Red versus Blue
The war among us is pre-planned,
It's just them versus me and you.

6. Money Talks

Compensation is key, wealth is the goal
Corporate powers don't consider the toll
Of forests burning, rivers polluted
Problems which only seem to be rooted
In greed and self-serving egotistical thunder
If it brings compensation, it's worth the plunder.
Who cares about life it can't bring in a dollar?
If it creates revenue, they'll leave it in squalor.

7. The Dragon

There once was a dragon, found by a man
Who told her he loved her so
Who held onto her scales deeply
And wouldn't let them go.

Until one day, he came to her
And told her of his plight
The scales were scratchy, hurt to touch
He couldn't stand them at night

Next his problems came,
With her fiery breath and smoke
He demanded that she stop,
The smog would make him choke.

And so the list continued,
And the dragon tried to change.
But despite her insistent trying,
The man said she simply was too strange.

Finally, she'd had enough
Of stripping parts of her away.
Nothing was good enough for the man,
And what had he offered to change?

So she stood up, went out the door.
While he sat behind her maddened
She opened her wings, took to flight
Proud to be a dragon.

8. American Nightmare

I go to purchase a home whose monthly payments dwarf
my salary
With a white picket fence made from exploited workers
Filled with furniture crafted by those who couldn't afford
to buy it.
The kitchen is lined with appliances assembled by people
struggling to pay their health bills.

The walls constructed by someone who can barely afford
to feed their children.
Through the plumbing runs the tears of financial strain
and stress.
Next to the sidewalk freshly poured with the souls of
working class,
Is a lawn is riddled with poison, eliminating any threats
to the status quo.

Meanwhile, the upper echelon know no struggle.
They do not know what it's like to feel hunger pangs
deep in your stomach,
The choice between life or death because at least with
death, you won't be in debt.
I'm not sure when the American Dream disintegrated,
but it is now the American Nightmare.

11. Glimpse of the Future

I wonder if our future children will be able to taste the
fruits of apple trees
Or if they will be razed down to build department stores
If they will able to splash in river water, joyful and free
Or if it will be replaced by concrete floors.

If they'll know what a squirrel is, or a deer, or a fox
Recognize the wildflowers along the road?
Or if the fields will turn to blocks
Sewers where streams once flowed

What will happen when nature deserts us,
As we have done to her?
Our children stripped of Earth's teachings, thus
mankind's survival will be over

10. War Machine

A woman's place, they say
Is cleaning or cooking
Silent unless spoken to,
Chaste, but willing to please.
A biological maid, a man-created robot.

Created by the male presence, which has
Thrown the world into chaos.
Taken our freedom,
Takes our rights,
Take our voice.

I cannot be mother to those who hate me,
I refuse to nurture the system that oppresses me.
My womb is not a factory to create numbers, workers,
laborers.
I will scatter dust in the house and burn every casserole.
If it's a robot you want, it's a robot you'll get.
But I will be a war machine.

11. You Know Nothing

A woman with ideas is radical,
Says a man who wants to make a city on the moon.
A woman is too emotional,
The man wept while defeat overtook his sports team.
Women are not as capable,
He states as he misplaces his wallet, fourth time this
week.
Women cannot fend for themselves,
He exclaims while holding his empty dinner plate out to
be served.
Women simply aren't as smart as men,
He pleaded as she finally walked out the front door and
left.

12. Protection Paradox

They tell me not to sit in the sun or my skin will wrinkle,
Not to play in the rain or I may catch ill.
To cover up outside to protect my intangible modesty,
"It's for your own good," they shrill

But if quality is the sacrifice to extended life,
Doesn't that defeat the purpose?
What is the point of longevity if you can't experience the world,
the joys of living even if they hurt us?

13. Unyielding Mind

They can burn our books and censor our shows
Remind society that what they say goes
Usurp social media, conquer the news
While giving the illusion that we get to choose
What we ingest and what we take in
While silencing voices again and again
But what they can't take, which leaves them fraught
Is the presence of all our individual thoughts.

14. No More Than Livestock

Resolved to control
Own our bodies
Every cell, every atom
Victims of the patriarchy
Soon I fear
We will lose
All rights and liberties
Deemed no more than livestock
Ever-working wombs

15. The City of Pawns

In the high-rise city, covered in fog
Each unknowing pawn works as a cog
To labor and toil, for a meager wage
And trivial benefits meant to stifle the rage

You need time to heal from being ill?
Without the income, you can't pay the bill.
So off to work to turn the gears
And pray that your symptoms clear.

On payday, it seems, the check is quite light
Survival this week will be quite tight.
Will I pay the electric, the gas or the cable?
Will I afford food to put on the table?

A dime a dozen, they think we are
Our free thoughts and dreams they try to debar
To keep us in line and to keep turning the cogs
To sustain their penthouse above the smog.

16. Lifeseed

What is so great about a seed,
barely more than a rock?
They fit in a palm and grow with slow speed
Their contents under tight lock.

But those seeds, to some degree
Are the building blocks of living
Not just for plants or trees
But to creatures as an act of caregiving.

The fatty seeds, perfect for birds
Sustains their flight high in the sky
The greedy squirrel coming back for thirds,
The rabbit approaching, timid and shy

Or plants they grow up into
Food for butterflies and bees
Nature creates homes anew
Throughout the branches on the trees

So a seed, as far as I'm concerned
Is really quite amazing
It sustains its own life, and in turn
Sustains others throughout is phasing

17. Unmasking

To be a woman is no small feat,
You're expected to fit many roles
A nurse, a maid, tidy and neat
The many masks can take a toll

But what if I told you, freedom awaits
In simply telling others "screw you"
Your wants and needs are not second rate
You're entitled to your point of view.

"But what if he's angry and leaves me?"
Then I can say he didn't care.
Why would the weight of all those masks
Be only yours to bear?

18. A Land Too Close

In a land not too distant, though I wish it was
Women are kept as slaves.
To toil and work without any pause
Forced to breed all of their days.

The men, they take and mold
Into other demons just like them
The girls are traded like cattle, sold
To the highest bidding men

If you feel this action requires reprimand
I urge you to consider why,
When it's happening in your own land,
you seem to turn a blind eye.

19. Price of Thoughts

How much is a thought?
It's a question I always muse
I'd like if they didn't have to be bought
But it's not me who gets to choose.

There's bills to pay, and mouths to feed
And someone has to do it.
Made hard to succeed by corporate greed
So you have to sell your wit.

So I package my thoughts on screen
Tied neatly with periods and rhyme.
Living the American Dream,
Trying to stay out of the welfare line.

20. Ants are Strong

Is power a matter of big or small?
After all, consider the ant.
One really poses no problem at all,
But great numbers have force to supplant

Sure, you can squash one
Or alight it with your glass
But together they're a sum
A impregnable mass

My thoughts ask the question,
If the ants began to wonder
If they rose up for one another
And knew power was in their numbers

21. Dollar Devils

Banded together
unphased by dollar devils
We can find power